PRAISE FOR

HOPE NO MATTER WHAT

Having gone through the devastation of divorce and seeing the pain in my children's eyes, I know firsthand the need for children to be able to express their feelings about what is going on in their hearts and minds. Kim Hill has provided a wonderful vehicle for doing just that, and added the reassuring promises of God for a little person's heart.

RUTH GRAHAM
Ruth Graham and Friends
Author, *In Every Pew There Sits a Broken Heart*

My parents divorced when I was a little girl, and I really wish there had been a resource like *Hope No Matter What* when I was struggling to survive those difficult days. I had the privilege of walking closely with Kim during the painful season of her divorce and watched her weather unspeakable heartbreak with unshakable trust in God's redemptive mercy. Kim is an amazing mom, a faithful friend and a compelling communicator. In short, she and her book are the bomb!

LISA HARPER
Speaker and Author, *What the Bible Is All About for Women* and *What Every Girl Wants*

Kim Hill doesn't shy away from the tough questions kids ask about God. When your children want to know "Where is God when it hurts?" this is a great resource. Kim's consistent answer is biblical and hope-filled: "God is right there with you." Way to go, Kim. You've given parents and grandparents a great tool.

MAX LUCADO
Bestselling Author and Minister

Kim writes straight from her still-vulnerable heart in this devotional for parents and kids who've encountered pain. Her insights bring needed hope—in digestible bites—for whatever stage of recovery we're navigating. Because she keeps her eyes on Jesus while processing through the pain and confusion, Kim helps us all move closer to the redemption God has in mind for us.

ELISA MORGAN
CEO, MOPS International

Kim is a *real* mom who has traveled the same path that millions of women have walked on—as a single mother. I have watched Kim wrestle with fear, grief and the simple hard work it takes to be an attentive and nurturing single mother. I pray that as you read Kim's book, you will be comforted to know you're not alone and find courage to use this powerful tool to bring God's presence into the lives of your children.

CHONDA PIERCE
Recording Artist, Comedian and Author, *Laughing in the Dark*

As I was limping through my parents' divorce, there were a few things I didn't understand. They were just way over my head as an eight-year-old. And while my mom was open to discussing things and helping me work through the process, there were still some things I didn't talk to her about. I wish I could have read something like this when I was going through that really tough time, because I think it would've helped. I think it could especially help younger kids during and after divorce to cope with their new situation in life.

GRAHAM SHULER
Kim's 14-year-old son

I love Kim Hill's frank, been-there, I'm-a-mom approach to helping kids face divorce and other hard things with which they are confronted. She speaks to children with a trustworthy voice and an empathic spirit and gives each parent a bridge to the souls of their hurting children, even as she gives their children a bridge to the heart of God. The connection is powerful! I highly recommend Kim Hill's devotional book for kids—any kids.

JAN SILVIOUS
Author, *Big Girls Don't Whine* and *Foolproofing Your Life*

Hope No Matter What will minister to children *and* to the child in the grown-up parent body. I received this book during a time in my life when I felt like every hard thing I've ever gone through—including my parents' divorce when I was young—came crashing to the surface and was trying to get out through a little, tiny opening. When life gets foggy and confusing, it is easy to forget the simplest truths. Come as a child with your child and be held by One who binds our hearts together and to His.

LISA WHELCHEL
Bestselling Author, *Creative Correction*, *The Facts of Life and Other Lessons My Father Taught Me* and *Taking Care of the "Me" in Mommy*

Kim speaks from a tender heart in this powerful tool for single parents. Her writing voice is just like her singing voice: enjoyable, entertaining, thrilling and life-changing!

JOE WHITE
President, Kanakuk Kamps

H O P E

NO MATTER WHAT

Helping Your Children Heal After Divorce

DOVE AWARD WINNER

KIM HILL

WITH LISA HARPER

Published by Regal
From Gospel Light
Ventura, California, U.S.A.
www.regalbooks.com
Printed in the U.S.A.

Library of Congress Cataloging-in-Publication Data
Hill, Kim.
Hope no matter what : helping your children heal after divorce / Kim Hill.
p. cm.
ISBN 978-0-8307-4515-9 (trade paper)
1. Family—Religious life. 2. Children of divorced parents—Religious life.
3. Family—Prayers and devotions. 4. Divorce—Religious aspects—Christianity.
5. Suffering—Religious aspects—Christianity. I. Title.
BV4526.3.H55 2007
248.8'45—dc22

Rights for publishing this book outside the U.S.A. or in non-English languages are administered by Gospel Light
Worldwide, an international not-for-profit ministry. For additional information, please visit www.glww.org, email
info@glww.org, or write to Gospel Light Worldwide, 1957 Eastman Avenue, Ventura, CA 93003, U.S.A.

CONTENTS

FOREWORD

After my divorce, several well-meaning people asked, "What about the children?" I remember that initially I didn't really know how to respond to that question. I knew I would have done anything to spare my four the heartache and wounds of these past years. We were all devastated. I asked the Lord, over and over, "What about the children?"

Eventually, His truth gave rest to my heart—the kind of truth that refuses to believe all the statistics or to settle for a broken-down life. And I began to answer that question this way: *I don't know what divorce will mean for my children, but I know one thing for sure: My children are covered by the blood of Jesus. He will be their protector. He will heal their wounds. He can make them into amazing people despite these circumstances. They belong to Jesus. They always have. He is the only hope they have ever had and I am sure He is still their best and brightest hope for the future.*

My friend Kim has written the most wonderful book about our powerful hope no matter what. Each day of this devotional is such a beautiful reminder to me and my children that we are covered by the blood of Jesus. The Scripture verses and interactive stories are a great way for me to keep reminding my children who we belong to. The family that lives and plays and rests under the covering of God . . . well, there is a hope that settles in that home. Kids start living the faith they had only heard about. They begin to see God's hand of provision because they are looking for Him. They learn to recognize His voice because they are listening.

I believe my children have actually weathered emotional lessons that have made them stronger. They are quick to believe God's promises because they have already seen Him work so mightily in our home. They step out where others might hesitate because trusting Jesus has taken away some of their fears.

This book is just the kind of encouragement your family might need to strengthen your faith during a weary time. So tonight, get all the kids together on your bed, even the teenagers who are so long their feet hang off (mine are 17, 13, 11 and 9). Wait until everyone is in their pajamas and it's almost time for tuck-ins. Play a game or something just to let them know this is not some kind of heavy we-all-have-to-do-our-chores meeting. Before you send them off to brush their teeth, tell them you found a great book that is about things we feel at different times. Then read Kim's first entry.

I promise they'll listen. And somewhere on the inside, they will admire you for caring so much about their hearts. And God will be there with you, covering your tender obedience with His mercy and grace.

Eventually this truth will bless your family: Our God gives hope no matter what. And when a home is built on that kind of truth, kids grow up covered by the blood of Jesus, and people just might whisper when they walk by, "It's amazing how great those kids turned out."

Bless you, my friend, and hug the kids for me.

Love,

Angela Thomas
Bestselling author of *My Single Mom Life*

ACKNOWLEDGMENTS

It's taken about six years for this book to actually come together.

Thanks to Don Pape for encouraging me to get it off the ground.

To Glenda McNalley, Susan Ligon, Steve Green and Melissa Riddle for fanning the flame.

To Wayne Brezinka for his amazing talent in trying to convey what it *could* be.

To Cheryl Green for great counsel and gracious friendship.

To Kim Bangs and the team at Regal for believing in this project.

To Lisa Harper for enhancing my simple thoughts into something worthy of printing. You really deserve much more credit than a "with." Thank you!

To Graham and Benji for allowing me to share our joys and pains in the hope that we can help others on the same journey find places of peace along the way.

INTRODUCTION

On September 11, 2001, our world changed forever. That night, my boys and I huddled together in a small, stone cottage and sang over and over again, "*The Lord is always with you, no matter what, no matter what.*" As I comforted my children with the truths I know about God's character, I was reminded that calamity does indeed clarify. Pain illuminates God's presence like nothing else.

As I'm sure you remember, fall 2001 was a tragic season for people around the world due to the awful violence of terrorism. But our family experienced a different, far more intimate, tragedy a few days before September 11 of that year: the tragedy of divorce. In no way can our loss compare to those who lost loved ones when those planes crashed into the Twin Towers, the Pentagon and a rural field in Pennsylvania. Yet it was still devastating . . . still *a death*. And unfortunately, the grief caused by divorce impacts millions of precious children whose faces will never make the evening news.

My hope is that this short devotional, which is intended for parents to read with their children, will be a part of your family's healing. My prayer is that God in His infinite grace and mercy will use these words (penned by a less-than-professional writer) to begin mending the wounds that divorce has inflicted on your family.

While I truly believe the *Hope No Matter What* interactive devotional has the potential to open the door to your child's heart, it isn't intended to be read every night for 31 days in a row. Based on my experience with my boys during the emotionally fragile time following our divorce, I recommend reading just a few chapters a week to give your child (or children) time to really process his or her feelings with you.

My boys are both extremely active (they roll out of bed at warp speed) and I feel like most of my affection, nurturing and guidance get sucked up in their vortex. However, at night they slow down and their hearts seem much more pliable, much more receptive. That's why I think bedtime is the ideal time to go through *Hope No Matter What* with your children. I recommend snuggling up each evening before bed—when hurting, insecure kids need peace and reassurance most—and reading one devotion aloud. (If you have children 10 and over, consider sharing the reading duties.)

Let the words of each reading be an opening for your children to express their feelings of fear, grief, anger or confusion. Listening lets your children know that they are important. If they are reluctant to talk, consider sharing some of your own feelings, appropriate for your child's age. Above all, let them know that they are not alone and whatever they are feeling is okay.

In each devotion is a verse from the Bible written in a kid-friendly style. Consider memorizing this verse with your children, calling it out to each other when one of you needs encouragement. Memorization is also a fun way to reconnect throughout the day, challenging each other to remember each day's verse!

As you create together in the activity section, emphasize God's goodness, love and faithfulness through the most difficult times in our lives. The last thing single parents need is something that complicates their kids' bedtime ritual, so I've tried to make the scrapbooking/journaling part as simple and low-key as possible. I've purposely avoided activities that involve searching for scissors or the right color of construction paper. Frankly, the whole point of the activities is to highlight God's love for your children and help them remember this season of their lives, *not* to encourage the Martha Stewart in all of us!

But when you have a few hours of daylight with your kids, I encourage you to flesh out some of the themes in this journal. For instance, instead of simply drawing a balloon or a kite, go out and buy some balloons or a kite, then repeat the scrapbooking exercise, setting them aloft in a park. I firmly believe that when you employ creativity and sensory experiences, the message of God's love, mercy and protection is more deeply ingrained in your child's heart.

Finally, at the end of each devotion, there is a prayer of blessing to say over your child. Praying for your children is a powerful way to show your love for them, and confirms that they are important enough to bring before God. After you have prayed, give your kids a chance to talk to God, too.

Over the past few years, as I have comforted my children with the songs this book is based on, the Creator of the Universe has reminded me that I am His child and He is with me no matter what. His providence will never take me or my children to a place where His love can't sustain us. And for that, I am profoundly grateful.

As you take your child's hand and walk forward one step at a time, I pray God's unexplainable peace will surround your heart and mind.

—Kim

SECTION ONE

HOLD ME, JESUS

the Prince at our House

Hold me Jesus
Cause I'm shaking like a leaf . . .
Won't you be my prince of peace?

FROM "HOLD ME JESUS"
BY RICH MULLINS

Have you ever seen a leaf shaking as a strong wind goes by? If you're watching a storm and you see how the wind blows things around, it can be scary. But if you're watching from a safe place, it helps take away some of the fear.

Sometimes we have storms that blow through our lives. Things happen that we can't understand. Things we don't like, that make us feel blown around and shaky. When a family goes through divorce, it feels like a great big storm. The wind can get pretty strong when that storm comes in, and we may feel like we're going to blow away . . . just like that leaf.

But there are safe places you can go when a storm comes. Just like a shelter during a hurricane, Jesus can be your safe place to hide and ride out the storm.

Even though God is mighty and holy and huge, His Son, Jesus, is called the Prince of Peace. Sometimes in fairy tales, a prince rides in on a white horse and rescues the princess just in the nick of time.

"Prince Jesus" doesn't always take us away from our problems, but He always comes to be with us in the middle of our storms, bringing peace in the middle of our problems. He was with Daniel in the lion's den, and when he and his three buddies—Shadrach, Meshach and Abednego—were thrown in a blazing hot furnace (see Daniel 3 and 6).

You know how you can't see the wind but you can feel it and you can see it blow things around? That's also how God can be.

We may not see Him with our eyes, but we can feel Him and see the way He works in the world around us. He can keep us safe when we run to His arms of shelter.

The Prince of Peace is with you, sheltering you from the storm.

I can lie down and sleep soundly because you, LORD, will keep me safe.

(PSALM 4:8, *CEV*)

Look around your room. Where do you think Jesus is while you are sleeping? Draw a picture of yourself tonight in your bed. And then, to complete your picture, draw a tight circle around yourself in red. And remember tonight, that is how close Jesus is to you right now.

Lord Jesus, please hold _____(child's name) really tightly in Your arms tonight. Don't let anything touch him/her except for Your love and peace. Help us to trust You even in the storm, and keep us from shaking.

Disarming the Dark

*When I wake up in the night
and feel the dark*

FROM "HOLD ME JESUS"
BY RICH MULLINS

I know that you can't really "feel" the dark, but sometimes doesn't it seem like it's possible? Almost like you can reach out and touch the blackness of the night?

Darkness can feel heavy, like a thick dark cloud from outside that someone let into your house. When it's dark at night, it can make you more aware of your fears.

And sometimes when either your dad or your mom no longer lives in the house with you, you may feel more aware than you ever did before that you need someone to protect you and your family. You may begin to worry about things that you never thought about before your parents got divorced.

It can really help to talk about those fears and to ask God for His peace. We can feel His peace as easily as we can feel the dark. He promises that He is near and that if we call on Him, He will grant us His peace.

It's hard to explain peace, just like it's hard to describe fear, even though we all know what fear feels like. Peace is just as real as fear, but in reverse. Usually your heart beats fast when you're afraid. Peace is just the opposite; your heart slows down and you feel calm—kind of like your body does when you lie down in a nice warm bath.

In Psalm 23, when David says God is our shepherd and that He lets us rest in green pastures, he's not just painting a pretty picture for us of what it will be like in heaven. David says, "Even though I walk through the darkest valley, I will fear no evil, for you are with me; your rod and your staff, they comfort me" (v. 4, *TNIV*). In other words, God is present even when everything's black and we can't see.

But just like David, we have to *choose* to believe that God is with us in the darkness, that He hasn't left us alone. We don't have to worry or be afraid. We just need to pray for His peace.

I will grant peace in the land, and you will lie down and no one will make you afraid.

(LEVITICUS 26:6, *NIV*)

Draw a picture of the scariest thing in your room at night—maybe something in your closet or under the bed. Then, take a walk with your mom or dad around your room, with the lights off and the door closed . . . but with a flashlight! Shine the flashlight on whatever seems scary in the dark, then explain what the scary thing looks like when you shine light on it.

Lord, please replace _____'s fear with Your peace. Help him/her to feel Your presence in his/her room tonight so that he/she can relax (like in the bathtub). Be real to us, God.

Blisters on my Heart

It's so hot inside my soul
There must be blisters on my heart

FROM "HOLD ME JESUS"
BY RICH MULLINS

Don't you hate it when you get a blister from wearing your new shoes before they get broken in, or from wearing a new baseball glove? We're all tempted to pop our blisters, until we figure out that popping them only makes them worse. It's much better to cover them up with a Band-Aid and let them heal on their own. Which never seems fast enough!

When we go through something hard in life, like our parents' divorce or losing someone we love, we hurt so much that it could be described as having a "blister" on our heart. Everyone around us might think we're fine, but we have something aching deep inside.

And as much as we want to get in there and try to poke that pain away, we have to give our hurts time to heal. We have to learn how to cry out to God for His help.

There's a really good king we can read about in the Old Testament named Hezekiah. We'll call him Hez! Hez had done everything God asked him to do, but then he got very sick and was going to die. He basically had a huge "blister" on his whole body! When he found out how sick he was, he turned his face to a wall and prayed to the Lord. Hez asked God to remember how good he'd been and how he'd tried to please God with his life.

Then this prophet (they were like preachers a long time ago) named Isaiah came along. After giving Hez a medical diagnosis, Isaiah gave him a more important message—one straight from God:

This is what the Lord, the God of your father David, says: I have heard your prayer and I have seen your tears; I will heal you (2 Kings 20:5, *NIV*).

God told Isaiah to make a paste out of figs (which are kind of like giant grapes) to put on Hez's wounds. When Isaiah obeyed, God completely healed Hezzie!

King Hezekiah's blister was on the outside where people could see it, but maybe you feel like you have one on the inside where no one can see it. You need to know that God sees it and He promises to heal it just like He did with Hez.

O LORD my God,
I called to you for
help and you
healed me.

(PSALM 30:2, *NIV*)

You may not feel like your heart has a blister. Instead, you may feel like your heart is heavy or bruised. Or maybe numb. With your parent or by yourself, try to describe what your heart feels like. Sometimes putting words to how we feel can help us feel less weighed down. In the space below, write a few words that describe how your heart feels tonight.

_____

_____

_____

_____

_____

Now get a few Band-Aids and put them over the words you've written down. Then pray the following prayer out loud: *God, please heal my heart the way You healed Hez a long time ago. Thanks that You are the same God You were back then and help me to trust You when I'm so sad and hurting.*

Dear Lord, thank You that You have promised to heal _____'s heart. Help us to be patient and let the blisters and bruises have time to get better. Thank You that You are with us even when it hurts.

Don't Forget

Well sometimes my life just
don't make sense at all
When the mountains look so big and
my faith just seems so small

FROM "HOLD ME JESUS"
BY RICH MULLINS

Reminders are great. I find myself buying Post-it Notes almost every time I go to Target because I use them all over my kitchen to remind me of little things I need to do.

I love it when God sends me a little Post-it Note that helps me remember things I know are true. One of my favorites of God's little notes is found in the book of Psalms, where God says that "the Lord is close to the brokenhearted; he rescues those whose spirits are crushed" (34:18).

Anyone who's experienced the pain of divorce in their home can be comforted by those words.

At bedtime, my boys and I like to remind each other that God is close to us and that when we cry out to our Creator in pain and disappointment, He hears us. He promises to be near us. As we talk to each other, the Lord reminds us that He is always with us, *no matter what*. No matter how we feel or how hard our day has been.

A few years ago, my oldest son, Graham, (who was eight at the time) had a few run-ins with the school bully. Several times at recess, when the teachers weren't looking or paying attention, this "bully boy" punched Graham right in the stomach. Getting hit was bad enough, but what made it worse was that nobody noticed him being slugged!

Our Heavenly Dad isn't like Graham's teachers. He doesn't miss anything that happens to you! He sees every single thing that goes on in your life, and He cares about all of it . . . because He cares about you.

When we remind each other about what we know is true about God, it helps us face the mountains (and even the mean bullies!) in our lives.

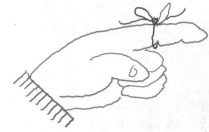

Is anyone crying for help? GOD is listening, ready to rescue you. If your heart is broken, you'll find GOD right there; if you're kicked in the gut, he'll help you catch your breath. Disciples so often get into trouble, still, GOD is there every time.

(PSALM 34:17-19, *THE MESSAGE*)

18

Design your own "Post-it Notes" in the space below. List a few of the ways your heart is broken, or some people who have "kicked you in the gut" lately (maybe just with words). Remind yourself that God sees them and is with you.

Lord, thank You for reminding us that You're right here in the middle of our pain and sadness. We know that we need You and can't make it by ourselves. Please give _____ the strength to handle the hard things in his/her life and to lean on You when he/she feels weak.

SECTION TWO

JUST TO SAY

thinking of you

I've been thinking of you

FROM "JUST TO SAY"
BY JAMIE KENNEY AND MATT MORAN

Have you ever seen one of those crazy TV shows where people race to see who can "count" the most sand? It's pretty ridiculous because if you've ever played in the sand, you know it's almost impossible to separate out those teeny-tiny grains.

Did you know that God says that He thinks more thoughts about us than there are grains of sand in the world?! Can you imagine how much sand that is? Can you imagine how many *thoughts* that is? (See Psalm 139:17-18.)

It's overwhelming to think that the God who created the universe—who splattered spots on leopards and stretched out the noses of elephants and gave beavers those funny "flapper" tails—thinks about us that much! Especially when you think about all the billions of people in the world, and that God thinks about *each one of us* more than all the zillions of grains of sand on the earth.

Whenever I go out of town and my boys are with their dad, I miss them so much. I think about them constantly. If I see a blonde boy at the airport, I think of Benji. If I hear Graham's favorite song on the radio, I think of the last time we rode in the car and it was playing. I think about them when I see football jerseys in a store, French fries in a restaurant, players on a ball field or anything else they like. Frankly, I can't go through a single day without thinking more times than I can count about my boys. And, as we've already talked about in this book, as great as a parent's love is for his or her child, it just doesn't compare to how much God loves us.

So, if God's love is at least a million times greater than your parents' love for you, and your parents think about you more times than they can count . . . how much do you guess God thinks about you?

How precious are your thoughts about me, O God. They cannot be numbered! I can't even count them; they outnumber the grains of sand! And when I wake up, You are still with me!

(PSALM 139:17-18)

What or who do you think about more than anything else each day? Write it down on the top line below. Now take the number of times you think of your special thing or person and multiply it by one million. Then multiply that number by another million. Based on your gigantic answer (which is *still* less than how many times God thinks about you), do you think you're ever *not* on God's mind?

_____

× 1,000,000

_____

× 1,000,000

_____

Dear God, thank You for being so concerned about _____, for always having him/her on Your mind. Help him/her to think about You more often too, and please help _____ to remember that Your love for him/her is way bigger than he/she can ever imagine!

a Song in

Gave a bluebird a song in G,
Said to say it's from me

FROM "JUST TO SAY"
BY JAMIE KENNEY AND MATT MORAN

Believe it or not, God knows you . . . I mean *really* knows you. He knows what kind of food you like, what kind of music you like and what you like to do at recess. As a matter of fact, if you pay attention, you'll actually begin to recognize "gifts" from Him.

Of course, I know you probably don't think what you're going through right now is a gift from God. You might not even think He's aware of what's going on in your house. But He is.

One time when my oldest son, Graham, was going through a really hard time, I had to go to Indianapolis for work and my boys went with me. Graham loves football and asked if we could go to a Colts game while we were there, but I told him we wouldn't have time. He was really disappointed.

The first morning, we had a little free time, so I decided to take the guys to the Indianapolis Children's Museum. On the way there, we noticed that all the streets downtown were blocked off, so we had to park the car and walk. As we turned the corner, we saw a big group of people gathered together. When we asked what was going on, they said excitedly, "The Colts are having a pep rally in a few minutes. All the players are going to be here signing autographs and serving Colt's ice cream!"

Graham couldn't believe it! He was hoping to go to a Colts game, but instead he got to meet his heroes in person! Later that night, we talked about how his foot-ball fantasy coming true was like a love letter to him from God. It was God's unique way of reminding Graham how much He loves him.

For you created my inmost being; you knit me together in my mother's womb. I praise you because I am fearfully and wonderfully made; your works are wonderful, I know that full well.

(PSALM 139:13, *NIV*)

The Bible—which is really a great big love note from God to us—says that you make God *sing!*
(See Zephaniah 3:17.) Take a few minutes to think about what kind of song you wish you could hear
God sing right now. And after you've decided what your musical request would be,
make up your own love song to God and write it below.

Dear God, we can hardly believe that You sing over us! Please give _____ sharper eyes
and ears so that he/she can recognize the gifts You send especially for him/her. And please help
him/her to really believe that You think he/she is awesome!

Wipe Your Cares Away

Raise your eyes to the sky above
Let me wipe your cares away

FROM "JUST TO SAY"
BY JAMIE KENNEY AND MATT MORAN

There's an old hymn my grandmother loves to sing called "Turn Your Eyes Upon Jesus," and it talks about looking up when life gets you down. The lyrics remind us that when we look to Jesus while we're in the middle of a mess, God will show us that our worries are small in comparison to how big and awesome and compassionate He is. Of course, turning your eyes toward Jesus when you feel like your heart's split in half can be difficult. Sometimes it's much easier to simply feel sorry for ourselves and hang our heads down around our ankles!

What that old song says is that we have to train our minds to think on good things instead of bad. Like daydreaming about swimming in cold, clear water when you're sweating buckets on a summer road trip in a car that doesn't have any air-conditioning. Or like imagining the fun things you're going to do on Spring Break when you're stuck in some boring math class!

But turning your eyes upon Jesus is a whole lot better than taking a mental field trip. Because when we take our minds off our problems and focus on our Savior, something *supernatural* happens ("supernatural" is a fancy word that means "something not of this world"—something that God is in).

The cool, supernatural surprise is that God promises to *lift our heads* if we come to Him when we're worn out, tired and don't feel like we can put one foot in front of the other. God promises to make our load lighter, to make our sorrow more manageable, to make our hearts feel a little less broken. When we choose to concentrate on Jesus and the good things He gives us, it's like a switch in our minds goes from "grumpy" to "grateful." That doesn't mean all the bad stuff will vanish in a puff of smoke—it means that God will transform our hearts from *hopeless* to *hopeful*.

Give all your worries and cares to God, for He cares about you.

(1 PETER 5:7)

Make a list in your mind of three good things that happened to you today, then thank God for them out loud. Now make another list in your mind of three things you are worried about tonight. Think about each bad thing, and then decide to think about good instead. On the lines below, write down what comes to your mind after training yourself to thank God in everything.

Thank You, Lord, for caring about _____ and for helping him/her to look up when he/she feels like looking down. Teach _____ how to look to You and be grateful when life gets him/her down. Give him/her a hopeful heart as he/she learns to trust You.

(Just to Say That) I Love You

*And that sunlight upon your face is
Just to say that I love you*

FROM "JUST TO SAY"
BY JAMIE KENNEY AND MATT MORAN

I don't know about you, but sometimes I take the good things in my life for granted. I expect to wake up in the morning being able to breathe, with the sun shining and the sky a beautiful color of blue. I don't typically stop to think that the sun and the sky are gifts from God—that He uses nature to remind us of how much He loves us.

But when I actually remember to look around and notice God's loving gestures, I'm amazed! For instance, have you ever watched a baby animal (like a puppy or a horse) start to walk just a few moments after they were born? Or have you ever seen mountains covered with snow on top—like giant mounds of whipped cream? Or have you ever really watched the sun set at the end of the day and counted all the colors reflected in the clouds? If you've observed any of those miracles, I think you'll have to agree with me that God is the ultimate Artist!

Our Bibles tell us that the entire world sees God through nature. If someone lives in the jungle and doesn't have a Bible or go to church, they can still know God is real simply by looking around. I mean, who else could make the stuff God does? Listen to what the psalm-writer says about God's creativity:

God's glory is on tour in the skies,
God-craft on exhibit across the horizon.
Madame Day holds classes every morning,
Professor Night lectures each evening.
Their words aren't heard,
their voices aren't recorded,
But their silence fills the earth:
unspoken truth is spoken everywhere.
(Psalm 19:1-3, *THE MESSAGE*)

Think about how incredible God is to create all the stuff around you. Then remember that *more* than all the birds or big trees or majestic mountains, God loves you best of all. Humans are His favorites of all His creation!

Thank the miracle-working God, His love never quits. The God whose skill formed the cosmos, His love never quits. The God who laid out earth on ocean foundations, His love never quits. The God who filled the skies with light, His love never quits. The sun to watch over the day, His love never quits. Moon and stars as guardians of the night, His love never quits.

(PSALM 136:4-9, *THE MESSAGE*)

On the lines below, list some of the things you see in nature that are clear signs
God is real and saying He loves you.

YOU!

_____   _____

_____   _____

_____   _____

_____   _____

_____   _____

Thank You for making everything around us, and for using things like puppies to remind us
of Your perfection. Most of all, thank You for loving _____ more than
the mountains are high or the ocean is wide.

SECTION THREE

AS BIG AS GOD

a Really BIG God

Nothing can shake you
If you're holding on to Him
Cause nothing is as big as God

FROM "AS BIG AS GOD"
BY KIM HILL AND JAMIE KENNEY

Have you ever wondered how big God really is? Is He as big as the tallest building? Or as big as a giant in a fairy tale? Or maybe as big as King Kong?

Sometimes at my house, my boys and I name all the things that God is bigger than. When we first started doing this, we lived in a house where my boys' bedroom was up three stories high. We imagined that even the angels, who aren't as big as God, were big enough to stand outside the bedroom window or even in a hotel if your room is on the twentieth floor.

Just thinking about how *big* God is seems to really help me and my boys. As I list the things He's bigger than, we're reminded that He's bigger than all of our problems, all of our cares. But the coolest thing is that He's not too big to care about some things that may seem really small to other people. He's not like your big brother or sister might be when they make you feel silly because you care about something they think is small. God cares about everything that touches you and everything you're concerned about because He cares about YOU!

God says that He sees everything. He sees the sparrow (one of the smallest birds on the planet) when one falls from the sky. He sees how hard the ants work to get their food. If He cares about these things, which seem tiny to us, we have to believe that He sees you and me. I know you'll agree that we are worth so much more to God than a bird or an ant!

Not even a sparrow, worth only half a penny, can fall to the ground without your Father knowing it. And the very hairs on your head are all numbered. So don't be afraid; you are more valuable to him than a whole flock of sparrows.

(MATTHEW 10:29-31)

Think about the things in the world that God is bigger than, and write down a few below. Now think about the things in your life that seem really big to you—especially things you're sad about it—and ask God to remind you that He's bigger than all of it.

_____ _____

_____ _____

_____ _____

_____ _____

_____ _____

God, thank You for being so big. Thank You that even though You're bigger than everything, You see us and care about the big and small things that touch our lives. Help _____ trust You to take care of his/her problems. Help him/her to put them in Your pocket and leave them there.

Nothing can Touch You

Nothing can touch you,
nothing but His love
Nothing can move you,
so rest in His arms
Nothing can shake you if you're
holding on to Him

FROM "AS BIG AS GOD"
BY KIM HILL AND JAMIE KENNEY

When I was a little girl, I thought that people who believed in God didn't have to worry about getting badly hurt. I thought being a Christian meant that you had this sort of super barrier around your body that made you impervious to stuff like broken bones or chicken pox or that gross virus that makes you throw up a lot.

But then I met Lisa C., a meanie who lived across the street from me in Mississippi. For some crazy reason, a lot of kids in our neighborhood used to come to our house in the fall to rake leaves. (I'm pretty sure the main reason they raked was so they could jump in the piles afterward!) Anyway, one afternoon, Lisa came to the raking party and got mad because there weren't any rakes left. She put her hands on her hips and demanded that I give her the rake I was using. I said, "No, I want to keep using it. You're just going to have to wait."

Well, Lisa didn't like that one bit. She said, "If you don't give me your rake, I'm going to rip it out of your hands and hit you over the head with it." Which is exactly what she did! I was so shocked; I couldn't believe she actually bonked me over the head with a metal rake—the kind with big spikes! I grabbed my head and looked at my hand. It was covered with blood. That bully had poked a bunch of little holes in my head and they were all bleeding!

Afterward, when I was sitting in the hospital getting stitches for the very first time in my life, I realized that I didn't have a magic buffer that would keep me from getting hurt. I found out the hard way that Christians get bonked and bruised just as much and break just as many bones as people who don't believe in God.

But the cool thing is that God goes to the doctor with us. More importantly, He promises us eternal safety and security in heaven, even if we have to get a few stitches or wear a cast while we're living on this planet!

The Lord's people
may suffer a lot,
but he will always
bring them
safely through.

(PSALM 34:19, *CEV*)

34

Draw a big kite in the space below. Now inside the kite, write several yucky things (like when some bully whacked you over the head with something) that you'd like to get rid of. When you're finished, close your eyes and imagine the kite floating up to God. He cares about every bad thing that's ever happened to you and promises to heal the damage done to your heart.

Dear God, thank You for promising to lead _____ through all the hard and scary things in his/her life. We're so glad You're in charge of everything and everyone—even bullies with rakes!

Too Much *FOR* Someone Your Size

*I know there's a lot that you
have on your mind
too much for someone your size*

FROM "AS BIG AS GOD"
BY KIM HILL AND JAMIE KENNEY

When my son Benji was little, he liked eating Happy Meals from McDonalds. He liked the tiny box his burger came in. He liked the little white package of greasy French fries. And of course he liked the toy that came with the baby burger! Benji loved that Happy Meals were made just for kids. The food fit him—not mommies or daddies. It was perfectly his size.

I wish life only handed out difficulties that were just our size, that we were never given a burden that felt too heavy for our shoulders. But life isn't fair, and sometimes kids get "adult-sized" problems to deal with. I've met more than a few brave children who have been diagnosed with cancer or who have lost a mom or dad in a car accident or who have had to deal with a parent who hits them. Maybe you've met someone who's going through hard stuff like that in school, or maybe you've met someone going through hard stuff like that in the mirror.

Have you ever overheard kids on the playground arguing about whose dad is the biggest or strongest? Boys especially seem prone to fight about their dad being better than someone else's! But the truth is that we all have the best Father imaginable watching over us from heaven . . . God is the ultimate Super Dad! He *always* comes to our aid when we're in trouble.

Whether trouble gets dumped on us because of someone else or we run into trouble because we did something wrong ourselves, God is always there to help us.

And when we're struggling to carry a problem that's way too big for us, God promises to lift the weight of it onto His own shoulders.

God will help you deal with whatever hard things come up when the time comes.

(MATTHEW 6:34, *THE MESSAGE*)

Next to each letter of the alphabet below, write an adjective that describes how incredible your heavenly Father is that begins with that letter. For example, next to **A** you could write *Awesome*.

A _____

B _____

C _____

D _____

E _____

F _____

G _____

H _____

I _____

J _____

K _____

L _____

M _____

N _____

O _____

P _____

Q _____

R _____

S _____

T _____

U _____

V _____

W _____

X _____

Y _____

Z _____

Dear God, You really are the best Father we could ever hope for!
Thank You for always helping _____ when he/she is hurt or in trouble.
Thank You for promising to carry the really big problems that feel too heavy for us.

Hole in it

You feel like your heart
has a hole in it
No one can see
Believe me, He sees

FROM "AS BIG AS GOD"
BY KIM HILL AND JAMIE KENNEY

When children experience their parents' divorce, no matter how old they are, it's a devastating event. When asked how the divorce made them feel, some kids say it felt like the world fell apart. Some say it felt like a tsunami hit their home and smashed it to smithereens. Some say it felt like winter came inside and made everything and everybody cold. But however they describe the aftermath of divorce, everyone who has had to deal with their parents splitting up will tell you that it hurts. (That is, if they're being honest.)

I have friends who were grown-ups when their parents divorced, and they said it still felt like the world was splitting in two. They say it broke their hearts and made them cry and wish things could be different. Even though they're adults, they'll tell you that they feel like they're trying to straddle an emotional canyon—standing with one foot on the side with Mom and the other foot on the side with Dad.

I guess in a lot of ways, divorce is like a death in the family. It's the death of a marriage, and everyone in the family feels the loss. It's the death of what God meant for a family to be. Our dreams of living happily ever after basically get piled into a casket and buried, and it's just plain awful for a while. And while God can heal the pain of divorce, it still changes things forever in our lives. That's why it's so important to allow yourself to express the pain, to be sad about it and not pretend you're okay when you really feel like your heart has a giant hole in it.

It's also important to know that you'll probably have other emotions besides the sad ones. One day you might feel like bawling your eyes out because your family isn't what it used to be and another day you might feel like punching holes in your bedroom wall out of frustration. I have a friend who goes outside and throws eggs against a tree when she feels upset about her parent's divorce—you might want to ask your mom or dad before you try that trick! Just remember that however you express your grief—whether you cling to a teddy bear and cry or hurl groceries in your backyard—God loves you very much. He wants to help you deal with everything that is going on in your heart and mind.

God, you see trouble
and sadness.
You take note of it.
You do something
about it.

(PSALM 10:14, *NIRV*)

Draw a picture in the space below of what you think God sees when He looks at your heart today.
Now write three words to describe some of the feelings that hang out in there most often
(for example: anger, fear, joy, loneliness, relief, sadness).

_____   _____   _____

God, thanks for loving _____ so much whether he/she is happy
or sad or mad. I'm glad he/she can be honest with You and doesn't have to worry about
whether You'll stop liking him/her or not.

SECTION FOUR

NO MATTER WHAT

Always with You

The Lord is always with you
No matter what, no matter what
The Lord is always with you

FROM "NO MATTER WHAT"
BY ASHLEY CLEVELAND AND
HENRY GREENBERG

For some crazy reason, we sometimes think that God only loves us and takes care of us when we're good—that God is like Santa Claus and His affection is based on our behavior. So if we say something mean to our brother or if we're sent to the principal's office for fussing on the playground or we sneak peas into our napkin at dinner instead of eating them, we think God probably won't want to hang around with us anymore.

Our idea of God walking away on days when we don't behave makes sense, because a lot of people are like that. Most of the time, people would rather hang out with us when we act nice. I sure want to be around nice people more than grumpy ones! And I'll bet you don't enjoy playing with bullies who hog the ball at recess, either!

Thankfully, God's love is bigger than "people love." He loves us *no matter what*. He loves us on our good days and our bad days. He loves us when we put our dirty clothes in the hamper *and* when we forget. He doesn't love us any less when we make mistakes. God doesn't just love nice, clean kids with families that look perfect; He loves kids who are dirty from playing outside *and* kids who are messy on the inside from the sad stuff that's happened to them—stuff that maybe no one else even knows about. Stuff that makes you feel like throwing a fit, or at least throwing your clothes on the floor!

We have to remember that none of that stuff—*none of it*—can separate us from the love God has for us. Nobody is strong enough to pry God's arms from around us. His hug is forever.

And I am convinced that nothing can ever separate us from God's love. Neither death nor life, neither angels nor demons, neither our fears for today nor our worries about tomorrow—not even the powers of hell can separate us from God's love. No power in the sky above or in the earth below—indeed, nothing in all creation will ever be able to separate us from the love of God that is revealed in Christ Jesus our Lord.

(ROMANS 8:38-39)

Rewrite the Bible verse on the previous page, Romans 8:38-39, in your own words and replace the word "us" with your name.

_____

_____

_____

_____

Dear God, thank You for holding on to _____ even when he/she misbehaves. I'm so glad that You won't walk away on his/her bad days. Please help him/her to remember that Your love for him/her is stronger than anything in the whole world!

Scratched Knees AND Scuffed-up Hearts

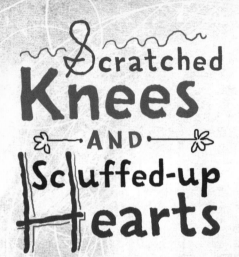

If you're hurt and bleeding
He can stop your bleeding.
Pray to God

FROM "NO MATTER WHAT"
BY ASHLEY CLEVELAND AND
HENRY GREENBERG

A friend of mine named Ashley is a really good singer and songwriter. She's super cool and creative. She even has a hot-pink guitar! Her kids are really creative like her. Her son, Henry, wrote his first song when he was only five years old.

Henry's song talks about those times when you fall down and get hurt and then run to your mom or dad and want them to kiss it and make it better. Even though their kisses can't heal your cuts the way medicine can, somehow they still make everything better. Just the fact that your parents will smooch a bloody, scraped-up knee or a dirty, stubbed toe makes your heart feel better. It proves that they really love you and care about you!

Our heavenly Father is even better than the best parents. And just like your mom and dad want you to come to them when you get an "owie," God wants us to run to Him when our hearts get hurt. You don't have to get all cleaned up before you run to Jesus either . . . just tell Him where it hurts and He'll make it feel better.

He can actually heal hearts that are broken in a million pieces!

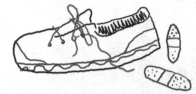
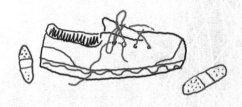

He heals the heartbroken and bandages their wounds.

(PSALM 147:3, *THE MESSAGE*)

Have your mom or dad help you pick out your worst three scars and remember together how you got each one. (For instance, the scar on your knee might come from the time you fell off your bike.) Now write a short thank-you letter to God for actually being there every single time you got an "owie."

_____

_____

_____

_____

_____

Dear God, please help us to remember that You're always ready and willing to help us when we get hurt. Sometimes when _____'s heart stings really bad, he/she forgets to run to You. Please help him/her to remember next time.

Your Best Friend

If you need a good friend,
He will be your best friend
Pray to God

FROM "NO MATTER WHAT"
BY ASHLEY CLEVELAND AND
HENRY GREENBERG

Hopefully you have at least one good friend; you might even have a *best* friend. Maybe it's your neighbor that you've grown up with or maybe it's someone you recently met at school. When we find a friend that we really like, we hope to have them as a friend forever. But because life is full of changes, friends come and go in our lives. Maybe you've had to move since your parents got divorced and you don't get to hang out with your best friend anymore.

The other day at church, my friend's nine-year-old little girl, Morgan, came up to me crying. She was so sad because her "BFF" (best friend forever), Clancy, didn't come to church that day. She only gets to see Clancy at church because they go to different schools. Plus, because Morgan's parents are divorced and she only goes to church twice a month with her dad, she only gets to see her BFF every *other* Sunday. So when she realized it was going to be two whole weeks before she got to see Clancy again, it was more than she could take.

I hugged Morgan while she cried and thought about all the difficult changes she'd been through recently. Her mom just had a new baby. Her daddy just moved into a new house. And she's started going to a new school. She basically has a whole new life . . . a life that's different from what she was used to. Now more than ever, she needs a BFF. And someone she only gets to see every other Sunday isn't going to be able to fill the great big hole in her heart. Morgan needs someone she can talk to and giggle with and cry in front of every day, a best friend who won't change even when her circumstances do. Who really will be by her side, forever.

You and Morgan can both talk to Jesus, just like a best friend. And He will actually talk back to you! The Bible says that Jesus is a friend who sticks closer than a brother. I love the "sticks" part because it reminds me that He's not going anywhere. He is the ultimate BFF!

Since God assured us, "I'll never let you down, never walk off and leave you," God is there, ready to help; I'm fearless no matter what. Who or what can get to me?

(HEBREWS 13:5-6, *THE MESSAGE*)

Write down three things you can do to be a friend to someone else. Now list three things Jesus has done to prove that He's your divine BFF. Is there anything on Jesus' list that people *can't* do? (For example, can your school friends be with you 24-7?) Write your answer in the space below.

How you can be a friend:

_____

_____

_____

How Jesus has been your BFF:

_____

_____

_____

Dear Jesus, thank You for reminding us that You want to be our best friend. We're so excited to hear that You will stick with us throughout our whole lives. Please help _____ remember that on hard days when he/she doesn't feel like he/she has anybody to talk to. Please remind him/her to talk to You about everything.

No Matter What

The Lord is always with you
No matter what, no matter what
The Lord is always with you

FROM "NO MATTER WHAT"
BY ASHLEY CLEVELAND AND
HENRY GREENBERG

When I was a senior in high school, we got to pick out a Bible verse to go along with our picture in the yearbook. I chose a paraphrase of some verses in Psalm 139 that said, "If I take the wings of the morning, and dwell in the depths of the sea, even there, I am never alone." I loved those verses, and I still love them! They remind me that God is always with me, no matter what else is going on.

Take a few minutes right now to read these verses slowly and "camp out" on what the psalm-writer is saying about God:

Is there anyplace I can go to
avoid your Spirit?
to be out of your sight?
If I climb to the sky, you're there!
If I go underground, you're there!
If I flew on morning's wings
to the far western horizon,
You'd find me in a minute—
You're already there waiting!
(Psalm 139:7-10, *THE MESSAGE*)

It's easy to forget that we're never out of God's sight. My son Benji used to try to hide from me when he snuck some M&Ms from the candy jar, but then he'd come to me later and confess his crime, fearing that I would count the M&Ms and realize he'd taken some. I guess he thought I had a "candid candy camera" in the kitchen that recorded his sugar thievery!

Sometimes we try to hide from God, like Adam and Eve did in the Garden of Eden when they disobeyed God, or like Benjamin did when he pilfered a few M&Ms—but we can't! No matter where we go or what we do, God is always right by our side. Which is bad news if you're a candy thief, but *great news* if you're afraid that God might abandon you, or if you worry that your problems are so big that they might somehow hide you from God.

This is my command— be strong and courageous! Do not be afraid or discouraged. For the Lord your God is with you wherever you go.

(JOSHUA 1:9)

On the three tiny lines below, list three things you're most tempted to hide.
Then in the blank space below the small lines, write, "Nothing is hidden from God!"
On the three large lines below that statement, rewrite the things you're tempted to hide
in great big letters, showing that God sees everything anyway!

God, thank You for promising to be with us wherever we go. Nothing is hidden from You,
not even our problems. Help _____ remember when he/she wants to hide
the things he/she does wrong that You see and love him/her anyway!

SMILE ON YOU

Alone in the Crowd

I know what you're feeling now,
lonely lost in a crowd
I see inside your heart,
where the tears fall

FROM "SMILE ON YOU"
BY JAMIE KENNEY AND TOM LANE

When I was 11, my family moved from Mississippi to Memphis. Memphis was much bigger than the small town I had grown up in and I didn't have one single friend there. But after a few weeks, some girls I'd met at school invited me to go on a walkathon. I was excited to be included and begged my parents to let me go. They were hesitant at first because the walkathon was going to be in a section of town they weren't familiar with. However, when I told them that one of the girl's parents was going to look after us, they said okay.

The bummer was that about an hour into the walk, my new friends met up with some other kids who were doing bad things, so I decided to walk on by myself. It was pretty scary because even though I was in a big crowd of people, I felt completely alone. No one among the thousands of people around me even knew my name. And this was way before cell phones, so I couldn't call my mom and dad. I just had to keep putting one foot in front of the other.

When I finally made it to the stadium where the walkathon ended, I called home from a phone booth. I asked my mom to come and get me because the girls I'd started the walk with weren't such nice kids and their parents weren't around after all. Things got worse while I waited for Mom to arrive because the girls I'd walked away from came up and started making fun of me. They called me a "baby" and "goody-goody" and one of them even spat on me.

The only reason I didn't panic is that I knew I wasn't really alone. I didn't know any of the people around me, but God was right there in the middle of it all. I took a deep breath and asked Jesus to make a shield around me and protect me from the name-callers . . . and He did!

Say this: "God, you're my refuge. I trust in you and I'm safe!" That's right—he rescues you from hidden traps, shields you from deadly hazards. His huge out-stretched arms protect you—under them you're perfectly safe; his arms fend off all harm.

(PSALM 91:2-4, *THE MESSAGE*)

Draw your own personal shield—like the ones you've seen in a fairy tale or a movie—and decorate it with words and pictures that describe God as Your perfect protector.

Dear Jesus, thank You for being _____'s shield and Savior and Friend. Help him/her to remember, even when he/she is in a crowd where no one knows his/her name, that You know _____, You love _____ and You'll never leave _____.

More Than You can Imagine

*I love you more than your
mind can imagine
That's why I want you to know*

FROM "SMILE ON YOU"
BY JAMIE KENNEY AND TOM LANE

When I was in college, I went on a trip to Belize, a small country in Central America. I stayed in a real grass hut in the jungle, slept with mosquito netting over my bed, held a scorpion and ate dinner with a family who had a pet jaguar! I went there with some friends during my spring break to talk to kids about Jesus. Every day we played with the children in the village, sang to them and told Bible stories. Each night, we walked to the middle of town and put on a concert. Big crowds gathered around to hear us sing.

One night some teenaged boys from the local church asked if they could try my guitar. The boys didn't have much money and the guitar they'd been using was really cheap and cracked and was missing a string or two. But it was all they had, so they'd tried to make the best of it.

The minute they started to strum my guitar, it was obvious that they were much better musicians than I was. As I listened to them play, I knew I needed to give the guitar to them. But I still needed to use it for the last concert, so I asked if they could meet me at our "hut" the next morning to pick it up. I didn't have any idea those guys had to walk several hours to get there, yet they didn't seem to mind when I handed them the guitar. They couldn't stop smiling even when we were saying goodbye!

Do you know the Bible says that God wants to give us good gifts, too? Not necessarily guitars or skateboards or baseball cards, but even better things, like peace and love and joy. And our heavenly Father loves us so much that He enjoys watching us smile when we receive His presents!

So if you sinful people know how to give good gifts to your children, how much more will your heavenly Father give good gifts to those who ask him?

(MATTHEW 7:11)

Write down the best gift you've ever received (for example, a birthday or Christmas present or just something special like a puppy). Now write down the best gift you've ever given someone else (for example, something you made for your mom). And finally, make a list of ideas about "gifts" you could give to God (for example, talking with Him before you go to bed).

_____   _____

_____   _____

_____   _____

_____   _____

Dear Jesus, thank You for giving _____ so many incredible gifts, like our family and _____ (ask your child to name whatever he/she is most thankful for). Please help us remember that all the good things in our lives come from You. And will You please help us to be gift-givers with the people we love, too?

When Your Heart is Hurting

*If you think of me when your
heart is hurting
Think of me if love's been untrue
Think of me as your friend forever
And I'll put a smile on you*

FROM "SMILE ON YOU"
BY JAMIE KENNEY AND TOM LANE

Have you ever been so sad that you felt like your heart was hurting physically? Instead of a headache or a stomachache, you had heartache. That kind of emotional pain is what people are talking about when they say "broken-hearted." My guess is that lately you've come to understand that phrase more than ever.

I'm so sorry that you can probably relate to having heartache, but I want you to know that you're not alone. You're not even close to alone. According to the latest U.S. census (which is like a giant roll call in our country, when nosy people with clipboards walk around and knock on doors to find out who lives in every single house), there are approximately 21.6 million kids who live in single-parent homes.[1] And just like you, they sometimes struggle with heartache.

Sometimes they dread school pageants, like plays or recitals or graduation ceremonies, because they know it will be weird to have Mom on one side of the auditorium and Dad on the other. Sometimes they get worried about weekends and the holidays because they know they will have to leave one parent behind to spend time with the other. Sometimes they feel like their heart is being split right down the middle.

If you're reading this and you feel like your heart is breaking into a million little pieces, it's important for you to know that you're not alone. I know that doesn't take the pain away, but I think it helps to remember that tons of other kids are walking up the same steep hill . . . they're carrying the same heavy "backpack" that comes with divorce.

> I am weak and broken.
> I cry because of the pain
> in my heart. Lord, all my
> desire is before You.
> And my breathing deep
> within is not
> hidden from You.
> My heart beats fast.
>
> My strength leaves me.
> Even the light of my eyes
> has gone from me.
>
> (PSALM 38:8-10, *NLV*)

1. "Custodial Mothers and Fathers and Their Child Support: 2003," U.S. Census Bureau, July 2006. http://singleparents.about.com/od/ legalissues/p/portrait.htm (accessed November 2007).

Without thinking about it, guess how many kids you know from school or your neighborhood or sports teams who either live with one parent or in a family with a stepparent. Write down your guess on the first line below. Now take a few minutes to count up all those kids. Write that number on the second line below. Was the actual number higher or lower than your guess?

_____

_____

God, thanks for reminding _____ that he/she is not the only kid carrying the heavy "backpack" of divorce. Please give him/her the strength he/she needs for each day, especially right now during this hard time. Thank You for hearing us tonight.

Your Forever Friend

And friends who are a part
of your soul
Some will stay and some will go
I'm gonna be there like sun
in the morning
A star that shines through the night

FROM "SMILE ON YOU"
BY JAMIE KENNEY AND TOM LANE

In the Old Testament (the beginning part of the Bible), a guy named Abraham was called *God's friend*. Another Old Testament dude, named Job, talked about the days when God was his friend and camped out over his tent. And when Jesus came to Earth, He said to everyone who believed in Him, "I no longer call you servants; I call you friends."

In this life, you'll have friends who come and go. You'll have buddies in elementary school that you won't hang out with in middle school. Or you'll have friends from one neighborhood that fall away when you move to a new house. Most of us think that every friend we make will last forever, but that's not usually the case.

I can remember crying while saying goodbye to my closest friends when we all graduated from high school. I thought we would stick together like glue no matter where we went or what we did as grown-ups. But now, most of us only get in touch when we send Christmas cards to each other! The truth about friendships is that many of them are like fireflies: They burn bright and beautiful for a season, but then they fade.

Life is sort of like a giant relay race. Most friends only run part of the race with you and then pass the baton to someone else. What's so amazing about God's friendship with us, though, is that it lasts for the entire course. He stays right by our side until the finish line. The other really cool thing about having God as a friend is that He also has amazing supersonic ears that hear every time we're sad or need someone to tell our troubles to. We don't even have to say them out loud for God to know them.

Don't forget Buzz Lightyear's famous words: "To infinity and beyond!" That's how long God's love for you will last!

God keeps an eye on his friends, His ears pick up every moan and groan.

(PSALM 34:15, *THE MESSAGE*)

Draw a giant ear in the space below. Now draw several lines coming from the ear and write examples of the types of sounds you think God hears on a normal day.

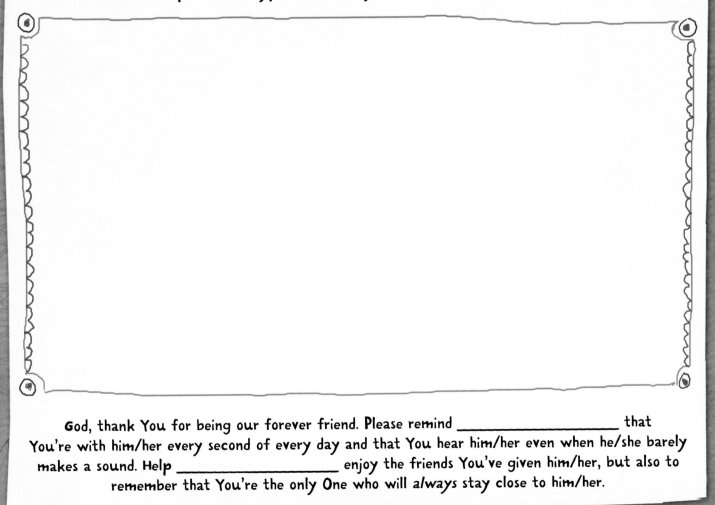

God, thank You for being our forever friend. Please remind _____ that You're with him/her every second of every day and that You hear him/her even when he/she barely makes a sound. Help _____ enjoy the friends You've given him/her, but also to remember that You're the only One who will *always* stay close to him/her.

SECTION SIX

CAN YOU SEE ME?

All Alone

All alone underneath the stars
I wonder if the shadows will ever go away
Where are you? Are you very far?
I feel you drawing closer
Holding me as I pray

FROM "CAN YOU SEE ME IN THE DARK?"
BY KIM HILL AND JAMIE KENNEY

Sometimes in our lives when something bad happens to us, our first question is, "God, where are You?" We feel alone and we think that if God was real, He wouldn't let such bad things happen. When all you've heard about God is that He's good and He cares about us, it's hard to understand why He would allow yucky things to happen. So we assume God must have looked away or gotten busy doing something more important, like naming a new star or something. But the truth is that God *never ignores us*. And there isn't any place we can go where God is not. Even though we all have bad days when we don't feel like God is with us, He's always there.

David in the Bible, whom we've talked about before in this book, also had lonely moments in his life when he felt like God was missing—when he felt like God had left him. He talks about his fears a lot in a book called Psalms, which is smack in the middle of the Bible. In Psalm 22, David cries out to God, "Do not be far from me, for trouble is near and there is no one to help" (v. 11, *NIV*).

Have you ever lost a toy? Maybe your teddy bear fell behind the couch and you've looked everywhere, but you can't find him. Or maybe you were convinced that some kid down the street stole your favorite baseball, until you found it under some junk in the garage! When you rediscovered that raggedy old bear or autographed baseball, you probably felt a little silly when you realized it wasn't lost at all—it was just squished behind the couch or covered up with other stuff.

In a much bigger way, that's how it is with God. He's *always* there, even when we can't touch Him or see Him.

There is no one like the God of Israel, who rides through the skies to help you, who rides on the clouds in His majesty. The everlasting God is your place of safety, and his arms will hold you up forever.

(DEUTERONOMY 33:26-27, *NCV*)

Draw three balloons in the space below. In each balloon, write the word of something "missing" in your life. The words can represent a stuffed animal that's lost or something more serious, like a friend who moved away.

God, thank You that You aren't hiding from us and that You never move away. Help _____ believe that no matter where he/she goes, You are with him/her and he/she is never really alone. Please help _____ to trust that You are right here in his/her heart, just waiting for him/her to turn to You.

Believe It or Not!

*Do angels come from far above
to stand beside my bed?
Did you really stop to count how
many hairs are on my head?*

FROM "CAN YOU SEE ME IN THE DARK?"
BY KIM HILL AND JAMIE KENNEY

There's a museum in Gatlinburg, Tennessee, called *Ripley's Believe It Or Not!* that has documented all kinds of unbelievable stuff. Things like women with long beards, men who can swallow swords on fire and people who can twist their arms and legs into such crazy shapes that you'd think they were made out of rubber! However, as entertaining as some of Ripley's exhibits are, I think our God does way more unbelievable stuff.

For instance, you've probably heard someone recite the verse, "God knows how many hairs are on your head." You may have thought, *Hmmm, I wonder if it's true, because I don't remember Him counting!*

"Hair math" is a funny way for God to show His affection, but if you think about the fact that God memorizes every tiny detail about you—I mean, even your parents can't tell exactly how many hairs you have—it's pretty cool! God loves us so much that He knows absolutely *everything* about us.

Another incredibly cool thing about God's love for us is that He sends angels to protect us. In Psalm 34:7, it says that, "God's angel sets up a circle of protection around us while we pray." So God not only does hair math, He's also in the "fencing business." In other words, He builds spiritual fences of protection around us when we talk to Him and tell Him we're in trouble.

You know, if you ask your closest friends to tell you the eye color of everyone in their family, they'd probably get one or two wrong—especially their brother's or sister's. We tend to overlook little details about other people, even the people we love. But God never misses a thing. He is intimately aware of *everything* that involves us. And that is truly unbelievable!

And even the very hairs on your head are all numbered.

(MATTHEW 10:30, *NIV*)

Try counting the hairs on your head. When you give up (before you fall asleep!),
write down three big or small things God knows about you that no one else in the world knows.
It could be something you're afraid of or something you hope will happen to you someday.

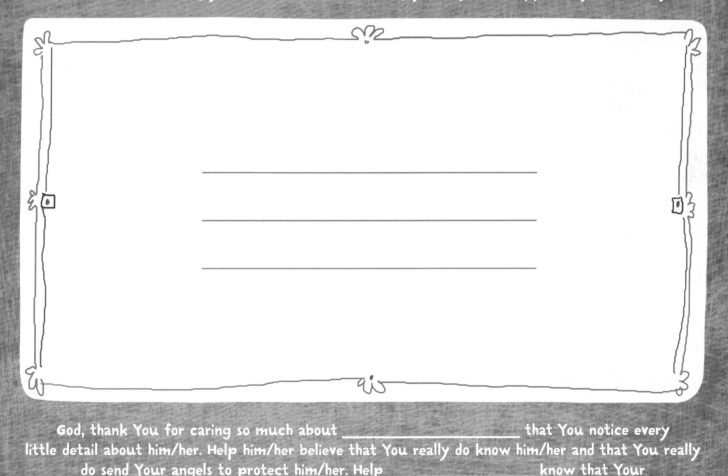

_____

_____

_____

God, thank You for caring so much about _____ that You notice every
little detail about him/her. Help him/her believe that You really do know him/her and that You really
do send Your angels to protect him/her. Help _____ know that Your
perfect protection is not just some fairy tale.

Do You See Me?

Can you see me in the dark?
Feelings I hide
Secrets I keep

FROM "CAN YOU SEE ME IN THE DARK?"
BY KIM HILL AND JAMIE KENNEY

Have you ever wanted to have a superpower? If you could, what superpower would you ask for? Would you like to be able to leap tall buildings and fly like Superman or swing through the streets and surprise bad guys with your web-spinning action like Spiderman?

Sometimes I like to imagine God as a supernatural superhero—one who's bigger and stronger and faster than all the rest. Of course, God isn't make-believe like Spidey—He's real! And the Bible says

His powers are way more amazing than some comic-book guy.

One of my favorite of God's "superpowers" is that He can see in the dark. He doesn't need special night-vision goggles. He doesn't even need a flashlight. He can see just as clearly in the middle of the night as He can in the middle of the day! Isn't that cool?

What makes God's X-ray vision even more awesome is that He can see everywhere, all the time. He can watch some kid snoozing in Africa at the same time He's watching you get sleepy in math class in America. That's more than my mind can imagine. Our brains simply aren't big enough to understand all of God's power!

God's supernatural eyesight takes in everything. He actually sees *inside* us. He knows what we're feeling and what we're thinking, even if we don't say it out loud.

On those days when you feel like you are invisible to everyone else, remember that God never looks away from you. He keeps watching because He loves you very, very much.

Then I said to myself, "Oh, he even sees me in the dark! At night I'm immersed in the light!" It's a fact: darkness isn't dark to you; night and day, darkness and light, they're all the same to you.

(PSALM 139:12, *THE MESSAGE*)

What do you think God saw when He was watching you today? List the top three things you're glad God noticed about you. Then write down one thing you wish God hadn't seen you do today.

_____   _____

_____

_____

Dear Heavenly Dad, please forgive us for sometimes forgetting that You're always watching over us.
Help us to remember that You don't ever close Your eyes.
You don't even have to sleep! Teach us to trust in Your super-vision.

Secrets i Keep

Feelings I hide, secrets I keep
Every dream I treasure,
can you see inside my heart?
Whenever I cry, whenever I fear,
I hope that you can find me here

FROM "CAN YOU SEE ME IN THE DARK?"
BY KIM HILL AND JAMIE KENNEY

Secrets can be fun. It's fun to be part of planning a surprise birthday party or keeping someone's Christmas present a secret until the big day! When I was little, my cousins and I had special American Indian names. We only used them when we were playing at our grandparents' house in Florida. Our names represented something in our personalities. For instance, I had a booming voice and talked a lot, so my secret Indian name was "Loud Drum." (My youngest son, Benji, is following in my footsteps. He doesn't have much of an "inside voice" either!)

Some of the secrets you keep are probably like our Indian names . . . they're harmless and fun. But you may be keeping certain secrets that you don't need to keep and that aren't harmless at all. Maybe you're hiding the fact that you're really sad about your parents' divorce. Or maybe someone has hurt you and then said that you can't tell anybody else what happened. Those aren't harmless secrets. Those secrets need to be told.

Spend some time thinking about an adult who is a safe person in your world, someone you can trust with scary stuff. Maybe it's a teacher or an aunt or uncle or one of your parents. Ask them if they'll go for a walk with you because you need to tell them something that's been bothering you. Then don't be afraid to tell the truth, because adults who really love you don't want you to keep harmful secrets.

Remember, too, that nothing is hidden from God. He knows everything done in private and definitely doesn't want you to hold something back that could damage your heart.

God would surely have known it, for He knows the secrets of every heart.

(PSALM 44:21)

Make a list of all the people in your immediate family (your mom, dad, brothers and sisters). Now with your mom's or dad's help, come up with a secret Indian name for each person in your family. For instance, if you have a big sister who talks on her cell phone all the time, her Indian name might be "Chattering Creek."

Dear Jesus, I'm so glad You're never surprised by anything. I'm glad You know every one of _____'s secrets—even the embarrassing ones—and still love him/her more than anything in the whole world!

SECTION SEVEN

HE'LL TAKE CARE OF YOU

Wipe that Tear

Wipe that tear from your eye
Don't you be scared of the dark

FROM "HE'LL TAKE CARE OF YOU"
BY DAVID MEECE

A few years ago, I was in Israel and saw these really cool little bottles for sale in some of the outdoor markets. They were shaped like a "genie" bottle, but were much smaller. I was so intrigued by them that I approached one of the shopkeepers and asked him what they were used for. He told me they were meant to serve as reminders that "God promises to keep our tears in His bottle."

You may not be familiar with that verse from the Psalms: "You keep track of all my sorrows. You have collected all my tears in your bottle. You have recorded each one in your book" (56:8) I think it makes a wonderful point—that God keeps track of every single tear we cry. Not one drop is unaccounted for.

I didn't remember hearing that verse very often when I was younger, so the first time I heard it, it was such a comfort to realize that God literally counts the tears I cry. Kind of like the way my boys keep track of the statistics of their favorite sports teams, God keeps a detailed record of the sadness that spills over and rolls down our cheeks. He does know about the pain you carry in your heart. Even the tears you cry in private are recorded in your heavenly Father's book.

My guess is that you've been crying more than usual lately because of your parents' divorce. You might wait until you're alone in your room at night to let the tears fall because you don't want to make your parents feel guilty. You may have cried so much that you think you don't have any more water left in your body!

I'm so sorry you're sad. More importantly, God is sorry you're sad. The whole reason He counts your tears is because He cares about you. You are not alone.

God is our merciful Father and the source of all comfort. He comforts us in all our troubles so that we can comfort others.

(2 CORINTHIANS 1:3-4)

Draw one big teardrop in the space below—make sure it takes up the whole space.
Inside the humungous teardrop, write a list of everything that's made you feel like crying over
the past few months. Then read the top 10 "tear makers" out loud to your mom or dad
or whoever is reading this book with you.

Dear Jesus, thank You that because of Your compassion _____ doesn't ever have
to cry alone. Thank You for knowing all of his/her "tear makers" before he/she even writes them down
or says them out loud. Help _____ remember that You're right here, ready to wipe
each tear from his/her face and willing to hold him/her until he/she doesn't feel like crying anymore.

Someone to Watch Over You

*For Someone is watching
to guard as you sleep.
Protecting each moment you grow*

FROM "HE'LL TAKE CARE OF YOU"
BY DAVID MEECE

Remember when we talked about best friends in this book? Well, my best friend's name is Lisa. We've been friends for 20 years and still love to hang out together! One of the things I like about Lisa is her sense of adventure. She snowboards and skis and scuba dives and even rides a Harley Davidson motorcycle!

Lisa is also a big talker, and she has talked me into joining her on some of her wild and crazy escapades. One time she talked me into skiing down a hill, through some trees and over a jump. Needless to say, when I hit the jump I went flying through the air and ended up crashing and rolling partway down the mountain while my skis, gloves and hat were strewn all over the place! Another time, she convinced me to follow her on the world championship mountain bike downhill course in Vail, Colorado. Of course, the trail was way too steep for me and I had a spectacular crash. I sailed over the handlebars and once again rolled partway down the mountain, scraping a lot of skin off my legs in the process!

When my mom noticed all the cuts and bruises afterwards, she said I wasn't allowed to "play" outside with Lisa anymore. Even though I'm more than 40 years old, my mom still doesn't like to see me get hurt. She *loves* Lisa—she just doesn't want me to end up in the hospital in a full body cast!

You know, God is like that, too. He loves His kids and doesn't like to see us get hurt. In fact, He is *always* watching over us because we're His most precious possession. God knows that when you're growing up, you're going to have your share of bumps and bruises. Of course, if you end up doing an "endo" over your handlebars, He'll be there to pick up the pieces!

For He will command his angels concerning you to guard you in all your ways.

(PSALM 91:11, *NIV*)

Draw the coolest bike you can possibly imagine, complete with racing stripes, a flag and whatever else you like. Now draw a huge hand in front of and behind the bike, showing that God is always watching over you—even when you're flying downhill with no hands on the handlebars!

Dear God, thanks for being so concerned about _____'s safety.
Help him/her to try to pay more attention this week and not be so reckless so that his/her guardian angels don't get too tired!

Love You Forever

He'll take care of you
And love you forever and ever

FROM "HE'LL TAKE CARE OF YOU"
BY DAVID MEECE

Have you ever wondered about how long forever really is? Another word that has the same meaning as "forever" is *infinity*. Do you remember when Buzz Lightyear used that word in the movie *Toy Story*? He puffed out his plastic spaceman chest and dramatically declared, "To infinity and beyond!" And even though it's cute when he says it, his *Toy Story* friends don't really get what he's talking about. Because words like "forever" and "infinity" are hard to wrap our minds around. We can't really understand something that doesn't have an end.

But God says that He loves us with a love that will last forever. He describes His affection as an "everlasting love," which means that His love for us will never end. It extends to infinity and beyond!

My younger brother, Jamie, and his wife have three children, and they spend tons of time hanging out together and having fun. Frankly, I think Jamie's middle name should be "Fun" because he's got such a great sense of humor. He tells jokes and makes faces and shoots hilarious videos. My brother is a great big barrel of laughs! So you can probably imagine how much my kids enjoy spending time with their cousins. But once several years ago, when Graham came home from spending the weekend with Jamie and his family, he was unusually quiet. I asked him what was wrong, and he said, "Oh . . . nothing really, Mama. I was just thinking."

I asked him if he wanted to talk about it, and he said, "Well, you know how Uncle Jamie is such a great dad and he's always doing cool stuff with Charlotte and Holmes and Grayson?"

I replied, "Yeah, sweetie, I think he's an incredible father, too."

Then Graham paused thoughtfully and said, "But as good as he is, Uncle Jamie's still not perfect. God is the only perfect Father."

And I thought, *I'm so glad Graham's learning this while he's still little.* Everyone needs to learn the lesson that God is the only One who loves us perfectly. He's the only One capable of being compassionate to infinity and beyond.

The Lord came to us from far away, saying, "I have loved you with a love that lasts forever. So I have helped you come to Me with loving-kindness."

(JEREMIAH 31:3, *NLV*)

In the space below, draw a picture of two or three things that look like they go on forever (like the ocean or the sky or a super long highway). Now weave the words of the verse on the previous page (Jeremiah 31:3) into your picture as a symbol of how huge and steady God's love is for you.

God, thank You for being the perfect Father. We don't really understand how long forever is, but we want to believe that You will always love us so that we can face whatever comes in our lives. Thank you that _____ can depend on You. When he/she forgets how much You love him/her, will You please remind him/her?

While You Sleep

Someone is watching
To guard as you sleep
Protecting each moment you grow

FROM "HE'LL TAKE CARE OF YOU"
BY DAVID MEECE

Have you ever seen a movie where some kids are camping out and they pick one or two of the people in their group to "stand watch"? The "watchers" have to stay awake to guard the campsite and their sleeping friends in case a bear or a bad guy comes. Of course, usually in those make-believe movie scenes, the "guards" nod off and some furry bear or a bumbling bad guy sneaks into camp and that's when the fun begins!

Tonight, think of God as the ultimate *night watchman* or *bodyguard*. He never falls asleep and is always watching to keep your camp secure, whether your "camp" is a tiny apartment or a nice big house. Plus, when God keeps watch, He doesn't need a weapon. Or a flashlight. Or a buddy to help Him stay awake. He doesn't even need to sip Starbucks coffee to make Him more alert! God's flawless character and His concern for us make Him the perfect, non-slumbering protector! Which means we can sleep like a baby when our head hits the pillow each night, knowing He's on guard. How cool is that?

Now you might be thinking, *Hmmm, if God's always watching over me and is the perfect protector, then why have bad things happened in my camp?* That's not only a good question; it's a question that adults wrestle with, too. And while there's no simple answer, the bottom line is that bad things happen because we all live in a broken, imperfect world. *Sin* (when we do what we want to do instead of what God wants us to do) wrecked God's creation and made yucky things like divorce possible.

The good news is that trusting in God's guardianship helps us get through bad and scary times. When we remember that God is right there with us, watching over us, and that He will never leave us, it makes even the worst situation manageable. So tonight, when your mom or dad turns out the light, repeat this verse from Psalm 121 to yourself:

He won't let me stumble, my Guardian God won't fall asleep. Not on your life! Israel's Guardian will never doze or sleep (vv. 3-4, *THE MESSAGE*).

No test or temptation that comes your way is beyond the course of what others have had to face. All you need to remember is that God will never let you down; he'll never let you be pushed past your limit; he'll always be there to help you come through it.

(1 CORINTHIANS 10:13, *THE MESSAGE*)

In the space below, draw a picture of how you see God as
a watchman or a bodyguard in your room.

God, thank You for being _____'s guardian, his/her ultimate night watchman.
Please help him/her go to sleep tonight knowing that You are watching him/her sleep, watching over
his/her "camp." Please teach _____ how to trust You even in the hard times and
to see the way of escape that You promise to make for him/her.

UP TO THE MOON

Big as the Sky

I love you up to the moon
I love you big as the sky

FROM "To the Moon"
BY KIM HILL

I think a mom's or dad's love for their child is about as close to having real unconditional love as humans can get. And it's especially important for kids who go through divorce to understand that even though their parents may not love each other anymore, parents don't *fall out of love* with their children. Frankly, it's almost impossible for that to happen!

You may feel like the parent you don't see as often now doesn't love you as much as he or she used to, but distance doesn't have to change how much you love someone. Even if you stuffed me into a rocket and launched me to the moon, I'd still love Graham and Benji every bit as much as I do now. I'd still want to listen to their stories and tell them to use their napkins at dinner and sing to them at bedtime. Living way up in the sky wouldn't change how much I love my boys.

Sadly, there are a few parents who move away after a divorce and start new families and act like they've forgotten their old ones. If your mom or dad is acting like they've forgotten you, it's very important to understand that it's not your fault. *You're not the problem.* Your absentee parent's heart might be in need of a tune-up. Somehow their heart got all bent and crooked. It's sort of like their love machine got busted!

And while I can't imagine how sad you feel if you have a "missing parent," God knows and cares about how you feel. The Bible says that God cares so much that He actually keeps track of every single tear you cry. It also says that God won't *ever* leave us, even if someone who seems better comes along!

Be strong. Take courage. Don't be intimidated. Don't give them a second thought because God, your God, is striding ahead of you. He's right there with you.

He won't let you down; he won't leave you.

(DEUTERONOMY 31:6, *THE MESSAGE*)

Draw a picture of the sky at night in the space below, and make sure to include several stars! Now pretend that the stars are talking when they twinkle, and beside each star write a few words you think your heavenly Father would say to encourage you when you're sad. If your mom or dad says it's okay, say your words to God (at the bottom of the page) outside tonight. You can even keep your eyes open while you're praying and look up at the real stars!

Dear God, thank You for making the stars and the moon and the clouds and the sun and rainbows. Thank You for making our world so cool that we have to believe You're the only one who could create it! Would you please straighten the crooked places in my heart and in _____'s (dad's/mom's/other parent's) heart? Please help them to remember that I am just as special as a brand-new baby.

When You Cry

I love to watch you when you sleep
I love to hold you when you cry

FROM "TO THE MOON"
BY KIM HILL

When my oldest son, Graham, was really little, we used to play a game at bedtime to describe how much we loved each other. I'd say something like, "I love you all the way from here to California and back," and Graham would reply something like, "Mommy, I love you all the way to Santa Barbara and then up to Saturn and over to Australia and back."

It was obvious that my three-year-old's grasp of geography was already better than mine, so I decided to stick with my strengths and write him a special song to express my feelings! I sang the song to him every night and Graham loved it, until one day when I was asked to sing it at his preschool in front of his classmates. Then, when I got to the line in the song, "I love to hold you when you cry," Graham tried to put his hand over my mouth so that I couldn't sing anymore. He didn't want his friends to know that he cried.

I explained to Graham that while his friends played rough at recess, *everyone* needs to cry sometimes, including brave little boys and big, strong men. One of the most courageous guys in the Bible was a guy named David. Remember, he's the one who killed a giant bully named Goliath with one rock from his slingshot? He also killed a lion with his bare hands and led Israel in battle against other nations that didn't believe in God. But even though David was a warrior, he still shed a few tears every now and then.

God doesn't think it's weird when we cry. He actually says, "When you cry out to me, I listen." Plus, there's never a bad time to cry to God. David said that he cried "evening, morning, and noon" and God heard him every time. God cares about you just as much as He cared about David. So if you need to cry, don't worry about it—you don't need to be embarrassed. You just need to run toward God when you feel the tears coming.

But I call to God,
and the LORD saves me.
Evening, morning,
and noon I cry out
in distress, and he
hears my voice.

(PSALM 55:16-17, *NIV*)

Get a blue magic marker and draw a whole bunch of teardrops in the space below. Now write a couple of words beside each tear that explain what causes you to cry.

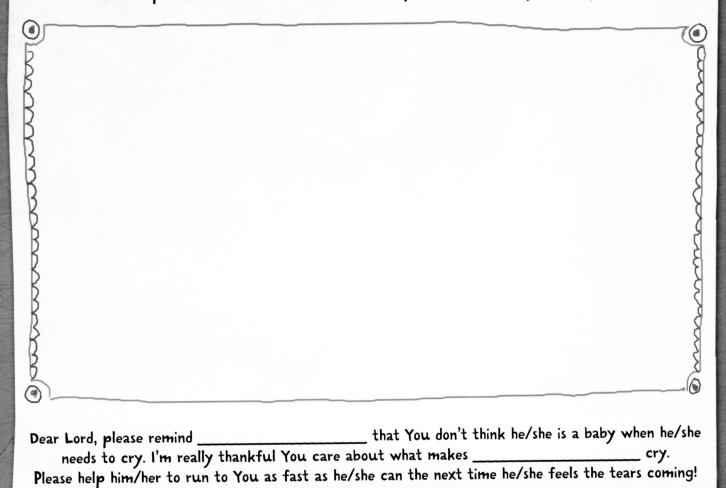

Dear Lord, please remind _____ that You don't think he/she is a baby when he/she needs to cry. I'm really thankful You care about what makes _____ cry. Please help him/her to run to You as fast as he/she can the next time he/she feels the tears coming!

I like a Tree

*One day when you're older
and taller than me
I'll say I watched you grow
Like a beautiful tree*

FROM "TO THE MOON"
BY KIM HILL

Have you ever seen a picture of a redwood tree? They're really huge—the tallest trees on Earth—and you can find them in California. If you've never seen one, you might think I'm making them up. They can measure anywhere from 8 to 20 feet across, and grow up to 375 feet tall! That's taller than the Statue of Liberty, from the base of her pedestal to the tip of her torch, and bigger around than a Greyhound bus![1]

Wouldn't it be awesome to have a fort way up high in one of those redwood trees?

Another cool fact about redwoods is that they need lots of misty days to get so big. Fog is their fertilizer. That detail may seem more weird than cool at first, but just trust me and keep on reading . . .

From the moment you found out that your parents were getting divorced, you probably felt a heaviness surround you, kind of like fog. Maybe right now it feels like the fog is so thick that you can't even think clearly. And you surely can't see through it to figure out what your life's going to be like in the future.

Even though you may feel confused because of the emotional mist you're experiencing, that fog is helping you grow, just like those giant redwood trees. The pain you're going through works like heart fertilizer—it will actually make you a stronger person.

Sink the roots of your heart deep into God's love, and you will grow up inside to be taller than Lady Liberty, too!

Dear brothers and sisters, when troubles come your way, consider it an opportunity for great joy. For you know that when your faith is tested, your endurance has a chance to grow. So let it grow, for when your endurance is fully developed, you will be perfect and complete, needing nothing.

(JAMES 1:2-4)

1. From "The Truly Amazing Redwood Tree," Treesofmystery.net.
http://www.treesofmystery.net/sequoia.htm (accessed October 2007).

On the left side of the space below, draw a picture of the kind of tree you feel like right now.
Then, on the right side, draw a picture of the kind of tree you want to look
like when you graduate from high school.

Dear Jesus, we don't like the fog that comes with divorce very much.
It makes us feel cold and wet and miserable. Please remind _____ that with
Your help, pain will work like fertilizer in his/her life. What feels so yucky right now
can help his/her heart grow big and strong.

How to Have a REAL Relationship with God

We've talked a lot through this book about God helping us through the hard times of life, especially times like divorce. But in the last book of the Bible, God paints a picture for us of what life will be like in heaven, a place where there won't be any more hard times. He promises that there will be no more death, no more tears, no more crying and no more pain. You won't even get splinters in your fingers or blisters on your feet! Things will be absolutely perfect, much like they were in the Garden of Eden for Adam and Eve, the first man and first woman God ever made.

Unfortunately, because Adam and Eve wanted to do things their way and not God's way, sin crashed into that beautiful place and messed things up for everybody. All of us, even "future generations" like you, were changed at that moment. Because of that original sin, we were all separated from God. God is holy and can't be associated with sin, and from then until now, humans have tried to find a way to reconnect to God. Some people have tried to get close to God by being good, by following a bunch of rules. Some people have tried to hook up with our heavenly Father by doing weird things like cutting off all their hair and living out in the woods by themselves. But God says in the Bible (a long letter He wrote to us) that there's just one way to reconnect with Him: by putting our trust in His only Son, Jesus. This is how the Bible puts it:

Jesus says, "I am the way, and the truth and the life. No one comes to the Father, except through me" (John 14:6, *NIV*).

Let me try to explain that in regular kid words:

Jesus, God's son, came to our earth in the body of a baby. That's what we celebrate at Christmas. He grew up into a man and lived a *perfect, sinless* life. He didn't make one single mistake, not even when He was hungry or tired! Then when He was in His 30s, Jesus allowed Himself to be killed by some bad guys and gave up His life as a sacrifice for our sins, which was God's plan to save us all along. Jesus died by being nailed to a wooden cross on a hill called "Calvary." Because He was perfect, the blood He shed acted like a big eraser

on all our mistakes. His precious blood washed over our dirty hearts and made them clean. He chose to be punished in our place because He knew we could never reconnect with God by ourselves.

The really cool thing about all this is that Jesus didn't stay dead. No way! The Bible says that after being dead for three days, Jesus walked right out of His grave. He miraculously crossed from death to life. That's what we celebrate at Easter!

At this very moment, that "resurrected" (a fancy word that means He isn't dead anymore) Jesus is sitting next to God in heaven, talking to Him about us. He's saying things like, "Isn't he great? Isn't she beautiful? Oh, if only they knew how much You love them!" He really wants you to know how much God loves you; He wants to be the bridge that reunites you with God.

If you want Him to be your bridge—if you want to have a personal relationship with Jesus—you can tell Him so right now. Simply say these words to Him. (You can say them out loud with your mom or dad, or you can say them in private.)

Dear Jesus, I believe that You are God's Son. I believe that You lived a perfect life and that You died on a cross to pay the price for my mistakes. I also believe that You rose again from the dead and are in heaven right now. Please forgive me for my sins and come into my heart. I need Your peace and Your perfect love. Help me to live my life from now on in a way that pleases You. Amen.

If you meant what you just said, Jesus is now your *Savior* (the One who saves you from your sins and from being disconnected from God), as well as your *Lord* (your King). It doesn't mean that you won't mess up and sin anymore; it means that you are God's child, even when you *do* mess up! You also have the Holy Spirit (who is kind of like God's special radio announcer—the voice in your heart that tells you when you're doing the wrong thing or the right thing in God's eyes) to help you choose to obey God, even when

you'd rather do your own thing. Plus, being a *Christian* (someone who's connected to God through believing in Jesus) means that one day you'll get to go to heaven and live forever and ever and ever in that perfect place.

Congratulations! I can't wait to see you there and give you a huge hug!

If you prayed this prayer tonight, it's important to write down what you did so that you can look back and remember that today, you made a decision to begin a real relationship with God. Make sure you include the date and any other details that will help remind you of the most important day (or night) in your life!

_____

_____

_____

_____

_____

_____

I'm glad to recommend the ministry of Kid's Hope,
which offers conferences in churches across the country
for children experiencing the loss of a parent through death or divorce,
and provides resources that can help your child through
the grieving process they must face.
You can contact Kid's Hope at:

P.O. Box 6020

Woodland Park, CO 80866-6020

www.kidshope.com

Surrender

Surrender is Kim Hill's latest worship project offering engaging new songs like "All To You" and "Open Wide" as well as worship favorites like "I Have to Believe" and much-loved hymns like, "Leaning on the Everlasting Arms" in her signature Memphis style. This cd also includes the theme song for Angela Thomas' new LifeWay Bible study based on the best-selling book, *Wallflowers Dance*. If you're a fan of the past three worship cds Kim recorded for Focus on the Family's national women's conference series (Renewing the Heart), you'll love this follow up disc!

Broken Things

Broken Things has been hailed by critics as one of Kim Hill's "bravest" projects to date. This cd produced by Paul Ebersold (Three Doors Down, Third Day) showcases her raw, award-winning vocals, rocking instrumentation, and deep messages pointing to God's goodness in spite of the broken human condition. These largely autobiographical songs resonate not only because of their authenticity and relevance, but also because the woman singing them has so obviously lived the lyrics, which brings unique beauty and maturity to this recording.

SPEAKING
Ambassador Agency
615.370.4700

Available at:
kimhillmusic.com
iTunes

CONCERTS/MUSIC
The Breen Agency
615.777.2227

More Great Resources from Regal

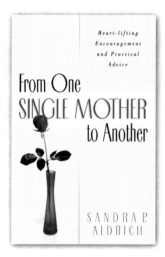

**From One Single
Mother to Another**
Sandra P. Aldrich
ISBN 978.08307.36874

**Release the Pain,
Embrace the Joy**
Michelle McKinney Hammond
ISBN 978.08307.37222

**How to Talk So Your
Kids Will Listen**
H. Norman Wright
ISBN 978.08307.33286

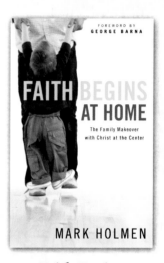

**Faith Begins
at Home**
Mark Holmen
ISBN 978.08307.38137

HOPE NO MATTER WHAT

Song References